This Book Belongs To:

With Love From:

Dedicated to Ellie & Oliva Wrage
May your heart for kindness always bring love and a little magic to everyone you meet.

The Christmas Kindness Kids

Illustrations by Jessica Wrage
Backgrounds and garland image produced by @DigitalCurio

Published by Ingram Spark
ISBN 978-0-578-57256-7

the Christmas Kindness Kids

Written by

Elizabeth Wrage

Illustrated by

Jessica Wrage

Be a Gift to others! Elizabeth Wrage

Wish List
Wish List

There once were two sweet children
who couldn't wait for the Christmas season;
to see what Santa brought for them,
was always their number one reason.

But then one day they realized
Christmas was much more than gifts.
There was a special reason
why we celebrated this.

HOLY BIBLE

It's in honor of Christ's birthday
why Christmas is so full of gifts
and being good because of Santa
means God's love is being missed.

Just then the kids decided
they wanted to share God's love too!
They knew that acts of kindness
would be a generous thing to do.

to do..

All throughout December
leading up to Christmas Day;
they practiced extra kindness
like making bread to give away.

They realized that some people
might not have many gifts that year;
so they donated toys to families
who could use some Christmas cheer.

GIVE AWAY BOX
DONATE

DOG FOOD

They wanted to be kind
to all their family too;
so they helped around the house
with little things that they could do.

It brought them joy to think of others
and little ways they could be kind.
The greatest part about it was
through their actions, God's Light shined!

Be Kind
Ephesians 4:32

You can be a Christmas Kindness Kid
each morning you awake;
and brainstorm with your family
a kind act you can make.

Then when you finish sharing
25 days of Christmas fun;
the best gift of them all arrives
we celebrate God's gift, His Son!

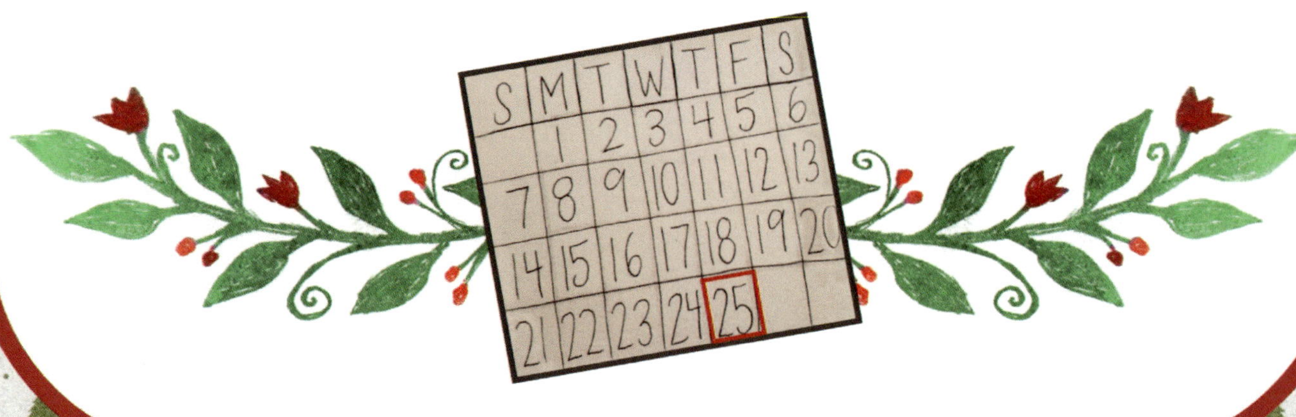

glory to God in the highest!

Let your acts of kindness
be a way to show God's love
and let the things you do each day
be a gift to God above!

A Note to Parents:

I wrote this book as an interactive way for my family and yours to enjoy the December days leading up to Christmas. The Christmas Kindness Kids can encourage your family to do acts of kindness for your home, neighborhood, and community. Donate clothes, bring a meal to a neighbor, write a thank you note to a teacher, or pray for your Pastor – the list goes on and on!

If you would like, get creative and surprise your children with a new idea each morning brought to them by the Christmas Kindness Kids. Leave a simple note "hiding" in a place for that day's suggestion and you're on your way to a new tradition of Christmas Kindness. {For example, tuck a note into a pair of shoes that reads "Let's find two pairs of shoes to donate."} Your children will love looking for each day's kindness idea the Christmas Kindness Kids have to share.

Need more ideas? Visit www.ChristmasKindnessKids.com for daily activity suggestions or to purchase The Christmas Kindness Kids: Kindness Idea Book.

Whether you read the book to spark kindness in your family or choose to engage in daily activities throughout December, my prayer is the Christmas Kindness Kids will help your family keep Christ & God's love for our world as the center of your focus this Christmas season.

Elizabeth L. Wrage
Author

P.S. —Be sure to share your fun socially using #CKindKids

Join The Christmas Kindness Kids at
www.ChristmasKindnessKids.com

- *Free Printables*
  { Including the Christmas Kindness Kids boy & girl pair to print, cut out, and hide with your daily notes }
- *The Christmas Kindness Kids: Kindness Idea Book*
  { 30 leave behind idea notes }
- *Ideas, Encouragement, and the Latest #CKindKids Products*

CPSIA information can be obtained
at www.ICGtesting.com
Printed in the USA
LVIC060136051119
636304LV00001B/5

* 9 7 8 0 5 7 8 5 7 2 5 6 7 *